POWER
Surfcasting

Ron Arra releases the cast that regained his National Championship in 1988—738 feet, 15 inches.

POWER
Surfcasting

RON ARRA
and CURT GARFIELD

 LYONS & BURFORD, *Publishers*

Casting sequences photographed by Patrick Wiseman.

Printed in the United States of America

10 9 8 7 6 5 4 3 2 1

LIBRARY OF CONGRESS CATALOGING-IN-PUBLICATION DATA

Arra, Ron.
   Power surfcasting / Ron Arra and Curt Garfield.
      p.   cm.
   ISBN 1-55821-112-8
   1. Surf casting. I. Garfield,, Curt. II. Title.
SH454.7.A77   1991
799.1'6—dc20   *91-13515*
                                                     CIP

Contents

Foreword

W HEN RON ARRA VISITED ME ON THE ISLAND OF MAR-
tha's vineyard a couple of years ago to dem-
onstrate the surf casting technique that had led him to
a series of national championships, my brother Dan
and I were hard-pressed to find a mowed field that was
long enough for him to do his stuff. There were plenty
of 200-yarders, but we knew—if Ron was in top
form—that we needed an additional 100 or 150 feet if
his casting weight wasn't to sail off into the scrub oaks.

We located such a field. Ron arrived on a dark, cold
windy day. The weather was so nasty that we didn't
spend much more than two hours out of doors. That
was, however, time enough for Ron to uncork several
long heaves including one that landed among some
grazing Canada geese about 700 feet away.

Among other things, that short session taught me
that he who practices long distance casting on dry land
spends most of his time walking and cranking in line.
The casting weight is often buried in the earth and
even if that doesn't happen you usually can't reel it
back across tangled grass and stubble.

I do my practice casting over water, and, save for the
few who might wish to enter formal competition, I sus-
pect that most of the readers of this book will do the

same. You won't be able to actually measure the distances you are achieving, but rough estimates—to pleasure yourself you can always err on the high side—will suffice.

Every surf caster would like to reach out another 30, 40 or 50 yards. From time to time, the added distance will enable him to catch more fish and it will always impress his companions. This skill can be attained by careful perusal of this splendid little primer and a great deal of practice. "Power Surfcasting" also spells out what equipment is needed to achieve maximum yardage.

The heart of Arra's technique is a smooth buildup of power and a smooth release. Those who favor spinning gear can forget this—although their casts will be much shorter—and use a quick snap to propel the lure on its way, but in order to master casting with a conventional (revolving-spool) reel you have to develop a smooth delivery or you'll spend most of your time dealing with backlashes. One of the charms of the pendulum technique used by Arra is that it can be modified to deal with actual fishing conditions or your own crotchets. If you've been flailing the surf for 40 or 50 years, it's difficult to make radical changes in your casting maneuvers. You won't—with every watered-down version of the pendulum cast—be sending your five-ounce Hopkins on a 200-yard flight, but there's nothing displeasing in a toss of 120 or 150 yards.

If you are somewhat reticent—as I have always been—about practicing a new casting method in front of fellow anglers, pick an empty stretch of shore and have at it. And don't be distressed if you fall into your old habits when blues and stripers are driving bait against the beach in front of you. At such a time, any heave that reaches the fish is a good one.

April, 1991   NELSON BRYANT

Introduction

I N THE UNITED STATES, THE NAME RON ARRA IS SYN-
onymous with long-distance casting. Ron Arra has
won four national Long Distance Casting titles and
dominated Distance Casting competition in this country for nearly a decade before he retired from competition in 1989.

This book is not intended to make the reader a Distance Casting Champion, although there is a chapter
on techniques and equipment for tournament casting.
This book's intent is to teach the surf angler a technique that will increase casting distance by at least 100
feet and cover more water with far less effort.

The successful surf angler may well say "Why
bother? I'm catching plenty of fish right now." Few are
the surf fishermen who haven't had an occasion to look
on helplessly as a school of game fish scatter bait just
beyond the reach of their best cast. Arra has helped anglers of all ages develop techniques that allow them to
cast further with less than half the effort of their original casting style.

Frustration at not being able to reach fish holding in

the middle of the Cape Cod Canal or beyond the Sandwich Bar led Ron to modify the pendulum casting techniques brought to this country from England by John Holden into a style all his own. Following the first round of the 1989 Stren Regionals, he became the first man ever to cast all the way across the Canal, a distance, at that point, of nearly 800 feet.

Ron has cast 850 feet unofficially on the practice field. His longest official effort was 758.44 feet in 1987 at a Sportcast USA sanctioned tournament in Falmouth, Massachusetts.

Reading this book probably won't make the reader proficient enough to duplicate that feat, although it's not out of the realm of possibility with the right equipment, 100 percent dedication and a lot of practice. What this book *will* do is help the angler interested in getting more distance select the right equipment and learn casting techniques that will get the most out of it with the least amount of physical effort.

Size, youth and brute strength take a back seat in importance to technique, balance, grace and timing. Anyone, of any size and physical condition, can learn how to cast for distance. It's just a question of letting the rod do the work for you. Turn the pages and we'll show you how.

1

The Right Gear

L ET'S GET SOMETHING STRAIGHT RIGHT UP FRONT. I'VE never hooked a fish on my 13½-foot Zziplex competition rod, and I couldn't land one with it even if I did, because the rod is too rigid from two feet below the tip to the butt end. The true tournament rod is designed for casting only and doesn't have the continuous flex needed to retrieve a fish properly. We'll talk about tournament casting equipment and techniques in a later chapter.

More and more manufacturers are producing blanks and finished rods designed for use with the modified pendulum casting technique that we outline in this book. They'll help you get your lure or bait to where the fish are holding and have a moderate flex action that will allow you to play a fish effectively once it's hooked.

For all-around surf fishing using conventional gear, I like a two-piece graphite or graphite-fiberglass composition rod between 11 and 11½ feet long with a medium-action tip—that is, one that has a gradual bend from midsection to the tip-top—and a flexible but firm

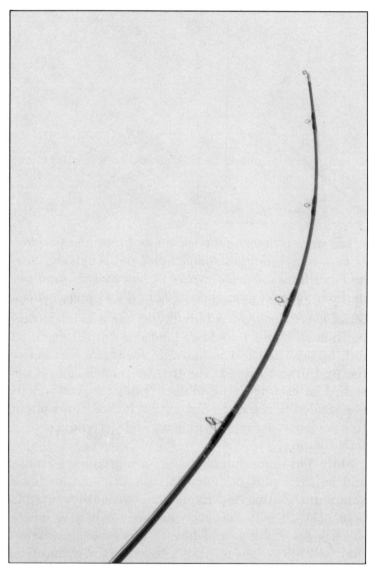

A parabolic action rod has basically the same action all the way through from butt to tip. This rod is ideal for fishing heavy jigs and bait rigs from four to eight ounces. Its continuous bending action makes it a good fish-fighting tool.

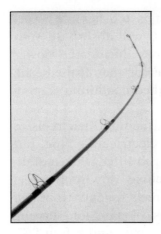

A rod with a limber-actioned tip and firm lower section is best suited for the modified and full pendulum casts and can handle a wide variety of lure weights from one and one half to four ounces. This rod is made with a graphite lower section and a fiberglas tip.

A fast tip action has most of its bend concentrated in the third nearest to the tip. This rod works well with the modified pendulum cast.

butt section. Beware a rod that is too flexible, especially at the lower butt section. It will absorb all your power in the cast, and never lock during the power stroke. A medium action is ideal for the off-the-beach cast and it can be used for modified pendulum casting also.

You'll see some surf anglers attaching their reels to their rods with hose clamps or electrician's tape, but for fishing situations, I prefer a rod fitted with a standard Fuji FS-7SB or FPSD "Deluxe" low-profile reel seat. This allows me to change reels quickly to adjust to fluctuating fishing conditions. Tough, long-lasting guides that don't nick or groove easily and a Fuji PST silicon carbide tip-top are also extremely important to have. I like the Fuji BNLG and BNHG series for use with conventional reels and the GBSVLG for spinning.

There are several excellent reels on the market that work well with the modified pendulum technique. My personal favorite for general fishing conditions is the 6500C from Garcia, a great distance reel with an innovative Ultra Cast design in which the spool rotates around the spindle on ball bearings. If I'm tossing big plugs in the two- to five-ounce range, I'll move up to the Garcia 7000 which is a great night-fishing reel because of its level-wind feature. The Newell P220 is one of my favorite jigging reels and the rugged Penn 140 is an excellent choice for casting heavier bait rigs. It will take a ton of abuse.

While I'll use spinning gear and the 5500C Abu revolving-spool reel with ultra-light lures, casting any lure or bait weighing one ounce or more calls for conventional revolving-spool reels. The Penn 550SS and the new Ultra Cast Abu Cardinal #4 are excellent saltwater spinning reels for casting very light lures. On these reels I use 12- to 15-pound-test line with about 18 inches of 20-pound-test leader.

On larger reels such as the P220 Newell, 7000 Abu or

Here are some conventional revolving-spool reels that can be used with the modified pendulum cast (clockwise from upper left): Abu Garcia 6500C Ultra Cast, Garcia 6000C, Garcia 6500CA, Garcia Ultra Mag III, Ultra Mag III side plate showing four magnets, Mag III Ultra-Cast spool, Penn 100 with plastic spool and Newell bearings, Ultra Mag III tournament reel with cork glued to adjusting mechanism.

Penn 140, fill the spool to within an eighth of an inch of the rim with a good quality monofilament. Most distance casting competitors use Golden Stren, but there

(1 9)

are other good brands as well, including Ande and Berkley Trilene and Abu Garcia's new Ultra Cast line. Top that with at least a 30-pound-test shock leader at least eight feet longer than the length of your rod. Ideally there should be seven feet of leader between the lure and your rod tip and at least three turns of the leader around the reel spool. I tie on a simple snap to facilitate changing lures because I think it gives the lure a better action. If I'm using a jig and live eels, I'll tie a swivel two and one half feet ahead of the lure to cut down on line twist.

While John Holden developed the pendulum technique in England primarily for bait fishermen, most

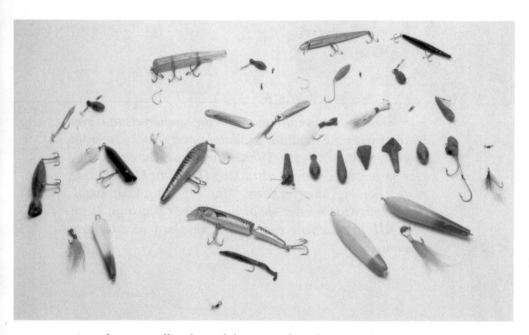

Aerodynamically shaped lures and sinkers work best for power surfcasting, especially where you are dealing with brisk winds. Hopkins, Creek Chub, Gibbs, Polaris, Super Strike and Atom all make lures designed for distance.

power surfcasting in the United States is done with plugs—the more aerodynamically shaped the better. Some of my favorites are the Hopkins, Creek Chub, Gibbs Skipper, Polaris Popper, Super Strike Needlefish, and the Catch and Fetch from Atom. Obviously, there are others that will cast—and attract fish—just as well.

2

The Pendulum Principle

T HE PRINCIPLE OF THE PENDULUM CAST, WHICH JOHN
Holden developed in England and Ron Arra re-
fined in the United States, is similar to that of fly casting, using the momentum of the line (in the case of fly
casting) or the sinker to load (bend) the rod. In both fly
and surf casting, the angler maximizes the amount of
stored energy in the rod by driving against the momentum of the sinker or line and then releasing it just as
the rod starts to unbend.

In a true pendulum cast, the angler swings the lure
away from the direction of the cast and then drives
against its momentum to load the rod. Speed and
strength aren't important here, but smoothness, timing
and practice certainly are, since the key to pendulum
casting is moving the arms and the body slowly and in
sequence.

All the casts described in this book start out from the
same basic position. Imagine that you are standing on
the face of a huge clock with the target at 12 o'clock.
Position your feet shoulder width apart with your right
foot at 5 o'clock and your left foot at 3 o'clock.

The reel position on your rod should be adjusted so that your hands are also shoulder-width apart when the right thumb is on the reel and the left hand is on the rod butt. The best way to get the reel location right is to tuck the rod butt into your right armpit and then reach as far up the rod as you can with your right hand. That is where your thumb should rest on the reel spool.

You'll need a 30-pound-test shock leader long enough to give you the proper drop and still wrap around your reel three times. The purpose of this leader is to absorb the shock of the sinker or lure leaving the rod tip at speeds well in excess of 150 mph. On beaches where there are a lot of rocks or sharp shells, a 15-foot, 50-pound-test shock leader is a better choice. For most surf fishing situations, 14- to 17-pound-test line is adequate for the rest of the line on the reel. If you're using a heavyweight conventional reel such as the Penn 140, remember to fill the spool to within ⅛th-inch of the top. This will give better control of the spool.

The last and most important step is establishing the proper "drop"—the amount of line between the sinker or lure and the rod tip at the beginning of the cast. As you become more proficient and develop your motor skills, you may want to fine tune your drop, but a good starting point is to have the sinker even with the first guide, which translates to about seven feet of drop when the rod is held vertically. The longer the drop, the lighter the sinker will seem because of line stretch. Keep your drop on the short side until you've learned and developed the motor skills and other basics, and only then experiment until you find the length that suits you best. If you have problems hitting the ground with the sinker with a seven-foot drop, the rod is probably not moving through the correct arc. Shorten the drop a few inches at a time and see if this helps.

There will be more time to cast with a longer drop

because of the wider arc it creates, and a longer drop also allows the sinker to build up more speed. This will make more sense later on when you have mastered the basics of pendulum casting.

Now is probably a good time to go over a few other terms that you'll read a lot in the next few chapters. The two that are the most important—and to some the most perplexing—are the outswing and the inswing, which are the heart of the pendulum cast.

The outswing comes first. Once you've taken the basic casting position, tip the rod slightly to swing the sinker out at about 7 o'clock, taking care that the sinker doesn't swing above the tip of the rod. Nothing to that, right?

Now for the inswing. This is accomplished by picking up the rod with your right hand and pushing downward with the left hand, to swing the sinker back from the apex of the outswing to a position behind and to the right of your right ear (just the opposite, of course, for southpaws). You'll feel a little tug at the rod tip when you've done this correctly. Two other terms you'll be reading a lot are "locked" which simply means that the rod is bent or loaded as far as it can possibly bend, and the "lever position," which is a point halfway through the cast where the left hand brings the rod around at shoulder height and pulls down to start the lure on its way toward the target while the right hand acts as a fulcrum. This is actually a pull-down-with-the-left-hand, punch-up-with-the-right motion, just a fraction of a second before the right thumb comes off the reel spool.

There is no mystery to learning and executing the pendulum cast. There is no age barrier either. All it takes is a little patience and lots of the right kind of practice.

Let's talk a little bit about the right kind of practice. Constant practice helps, but constantly practicing poor technique will only produce bad habits and poor casting. The best way to learn is to practice with a partner, even if he or she uses a different style. A partner can observe your cast, compare it with the illustrations in this book, and point out faults.

Executing the field-type pendulum cast with full backswing is a goal for which every caster can strive, but not on the first day you pick up a rod. No top caster learned his or her style of the pendulum cast all at once. It took most of them many hours over a period of years to build upon the basics and form a good foundation of the proper motor skills.

The modified pendulum cast is capable of producing distances in excess of 525 feet on the practice field when perfected, but it's much safer to practice at the water's edge as long as there is nobody to your right if you're right-handed or to your left if you're a southpaw. It also has the advantage of exposing you to actual fishing conditions.

Use a 50-pound shock leader ahead of a 15- or 17-pound-test running line for practice. Tie a strong snap to the shock leader because the greatest wear generally occurs just above the sinker. If you practice on a field, make sure that it is free of other people. Crackoffs have been known to travel 950 feet or more and the sinker leaves the rod tip at speeds of close to 200 mph. An errant sinker can kill or severely injure an innocent bystander.

With any casting style, the direction of the cast will be wild to start, so bear that in mind when choosing a place to practice. Once you've attained some consistency, you can adjust the position of your feet so that the sinker goes in a safe direction.

No matter what style of the pendulum cast you are learning, the backswing is the most important. Get this wrong and you'll be unable to achieve a fully-locked rod. You can practice a proper backswing by dry casting in your back yard. The backswing should be very slow, smooth and controlled. Try to create a mental picture of floating on a cloud as you go through the motions. The slower and more graceful you are when you execute this portion of the cast, the longer and more accurate the cast will be.

Expert casters make the pendulum cast look easy, but don't get discouraged if you can't duplicate their efforts right away. We all were beginners at one time and the top casters have worked for years to develop their skills. Some people have natural coordination and get good distance with only a few weeks of practice while others are slow learners who often become better casters than the naturals. In either case, there's no substitute for dedication. Keep at it and you may find yourself going beyond your greatest expectations. Good luck!!

3

Casting
Techniques

OFF-THE-GROUND CAST

We're starting with the off-the-ground cast for two reasons. First, it builds confidence; and second, it allows the caster to develop the motor skills necessary for the pendulum casts that we'll describe later.

The off-the-ground cast is actually the final half of a true pendulum cast. It uses the friction of the bait or lure resting on the beach to "load" the rod. Before you start, establish your drop by holding the rod in a vertical position and letting out line until your lure or sinker hangs opposite the first (collecting) guide.

I'm taking up a good starting position, feet shoulder-width apart, the rod cocked behind me at a 45-degree angle with the bait or lure lying on the sand at a 90-degree angle to the rod. The target is at 12 o'clock and I'm standing with my right foot at five o'clock and my left foot at 3 o'clock. My knees are slightly bent and my head is up for balance.

I'm starting to pick up the sinker by pulling the rod forward with my body and both arms, almost as if hauling on a large rope. My weight is still on my right foot and my hips are twisted similar to those of a golfer at the head of the backswing. I can feel the pull of the sinker on the beach starting to load the rod and I'm starting to come around as slow as I possibly can—like floating on a cloud. It's important to keep the left hand at least at shoulder level. Otherwise you won't have the leverage you need later on.

My hips are starting to uncoil and my weight is beginning to transfer from my right foot to my left. My right
hand is pushing the rod up into the lever position and
my left hand is starting to pull down. The rod is now
fully loaded. Note that I'm not hurrying the cast. The
longer you can leave that rod behind you, the longer
the cast you're going to have. Let the rod do the work
for you and keep your head up.

I'm pushing with my right hand and pulling down with my left to bring the rod up into the finishing position. My thumb is off the reel, the rod is springing out on its own and the lure is on its way.

My weight is now completely on my left foot and I'm pointing the rod tip toward the target so that the line will flow smoothly through the guides.

The follow through. I'm letting the rod tip follow the trajectory of the lure as it descends to the water. It's important never to tighten up on a cast. Just move through it gracefully, using the body more than the arms. That's where you're going to get your distance.

THE MODIFIED PENDULUM CAST

This cast is a modified version of the tournament cast that has produced distances of more than 800 feet in competition. Nobody's going to get that kind of distance using conventional fishing gear, but with practice, anyone can add 100 feet or more to his or her best distance with a lot less effort than conventional casting methods. The tricky part of this cast is the timing of the outswing and inswing, which will take a little practice.

A selection of excellent salt-water reels that will work well with the modified pendulum cast. Surrounding the Abu Ultra Cast Cardinal 4 are (clockwise from left) Penn 150 Surf Master, Penn 850 SS, Newell P220, Abu 758 BW, Abu 7000, Abu 6500C Ultra-Cast.

I'm taking up a good starting position, feet shoulder-width apart, the rod cocked behind me at a 45-degree angle, the reel at eye level with my right thumb on the spool. I've established my drop to the first (collecting) guide. The target is at 12 o'clock and I'm standing with my right foot at 5 o'clock and my left foot at 3 o'clock. My knees are slightly bent, my head is up for balance and I've started the sinker on a slow, relaxed outswing, taking care that the top of the arc doesn't go above the rod tip.

The sinker is at the top of the outswing, in line with, but not above the tip of the rod. I'm starting to gently pull on the sinker by moving the rod to my right to start it back on the inswing. The ideal inswing should finish with the sinker a little above and well behind the caster's right ear.

The sinker is in an ideal position behind me at the very top of the inswing, just before the sinker reaches its highest point, and I've started to lean my body and swing away from the sinker's momentum very gracefully in order to load the rod. You'll feel a little tug at the rod tip when you do this correctly. That's the signal to start uncoiling your hips and slowly bring the rod around.

Here I'm actually starting the cast. All my weight is on my right foot and I'm pulling the rod through as gracefully as possible, letting my body do most of the work while my arms go along for the ride. I'm pulling the rod around with my left hand and guiding it with my right. The key here is not to rush things. Keep telling yourself to relax and take your time.

The rod is now fully locked (meaning it can't possibly bend any more) and my weight is evenly distributed on both feet. My head is up for balance and I'm letting my body do the work.

I've started to twist my hips to transfer my weight to my left foot and my arms are finally coming into play, pulling with my left and pushing with my right to bring the rod up into the lever position with my left hand at shoulder level. Meanwhile I'm bringing my body around to keep the rod locked and increasing speed gradually. Trying to rush things at this point is only going to bring on a backlash.

It's punch-out time. I'm approaching the release point, pulling down with my left hand and punching up with my right, releasing my thumb from the reel when my right hand passes my right knee. The key here is to leave yourself in a position where your body is pushing up under the rod, sort of like trying to punch out somebody who is three feet taller than you are.

Following through. I'm taking care to keep the rod in line with the trajectory of the cast so that the line flows smoothly through the guides for maximum distance. I'm also *very lightly* feathering the bell (side) of the reel spool with my right thumb to avoid a backlash.

THE WADING PENDULUM CAST

There are places all along the coast where the combination of a deep spot near the beach and an offshore bar make it necessary to wade out as far as possible in order to cast a lure or bait into the deep water on the far side of the bar where the fish are holding. In a situation like this the wading pendulum cast can get you into fish that are out of reach to conventional casters.

I've waded out until I'm crotch deep in the water and have established a good, firm foot position. Since I won't be able to move my feet much during the cast, I want to get as much traction as possible. Because I'm in the water I'm carrying my hands much higher and taking a much shorter drop than I would with the modified pendulum cast. I'm being careful not to let the sinker hit the water behind me on the outswing.

(4 9)

The sinker is just reaching the peak of the outswing in an ideal position—not above the rod tip.

I've pivoted to my right and started the sinker back on the inswing, taking my time and trying to keep my movements smooth and relaxed while maintaining my footing.

The sinker is at the peak of the inswing and the tip of the rod is bending slightly. When I feel that little tug I start turning my body to my left and bringing the rod around very slowly and gracefully.

My body is bringing the rod around as my hips start to uncoil. I'm pulling the rod through with my left hand and guiding it with my right. My head is up and my knees are slightly bent for good balance.

The rod is starting to bend and lock and I'm turning my body toward the target, building up power with very little effort. My hands are much higher than normal to keep the sinker from hitting the water and I'm punching up with my right hand while pulling down with my left.

My thumb has come off the reel and the sinker is on its way. I'm starting to finish up the cast by following the trajectory of the sinker with my rod tip.

The follow through. Here I'm keeping the rod lined up with the lure so that the line will flow smoothly through the guides. This cast won't produce the distance that a modified pendulum cast off the beach will, but with it I find that I can easily cast a three-ounce plug 300 feet. A limber-tip rod works best with this cast.

THE SLINGSHOT CAST

This cast doesn't really employ the pendulum principle, but it's handy to know when you're fishing on a crowded beach or have rocks behind you that would interfere with a normal modified pendulum cast. This cast is made straight overhand and starts with a much shorter drop than normal. Two feet is about right.

I'm setting up perpendicular to the beach and as close as possible to the highest obstruction behind me without its actually making contact with the rod, which is being held higher than normal. Good footing is very important here.

(57)

I'm starting the cast by bending both knees with the rod held high behind me and at right angles to the beach.

I'm springing up with my weight on my right foot and starting to punch up with my right hand and pull down with my left.

My weight is starting to shift from my right foot to my left. The rod is held high in the lever position and is beginning to load.

The release point. Note that the trajectory of the rod is straight overhand and not off to the side. The normal torso and hip swing of the modified pendulum is replaced by the springing upward motion.

Following through. The rod tip follows the trajectory of the sinker so that the line will flow through the guides with as little resistance as possible. This cast won't get you the distance that the modified pendulum will but it is ideal for use in close quarters where safety is paramount.

OFF-GROUND CAST

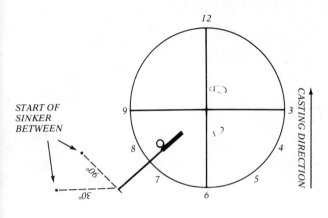

MODIFIED PENDULUM CAST

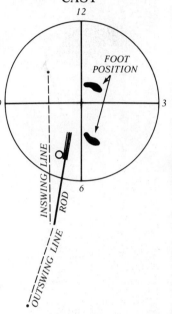

WADING PENDULUM CAST

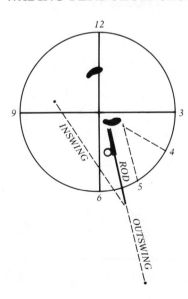

SLINGSHOT CAST

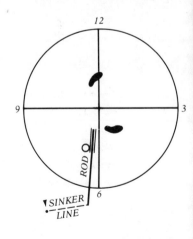

FULL TOURNAMENT PENDULUM CAST

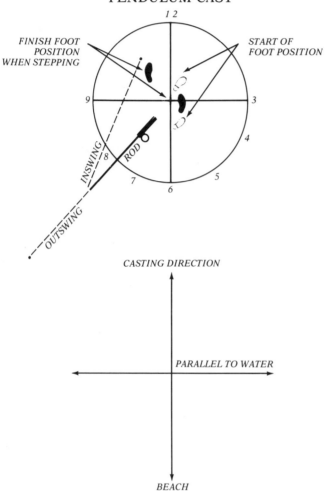

4

Taking Care
of Your Gear
and Yourself

I 'VE BEEN AN ATHLETE ALL MY LIFE, PLAYING BASEBALL, football and track in high school, and later playing professionally in the Pittsburgh Pirates farm system. The motor skills I developed along the way have undoubtedly helped me become a better caster.

While not every saltwater angler is a pro athlete, there are a few tricks of the athlete's trade that will help improve your distance. One of the most important is warming up before you cast.

I'm not talking about the kinds of exercises that you may have seen me go through with wrist weights prior to a Distance Casting competition*. You can loosen up just as easily by making 25 or 30 dry casts (*without*) wrist weights before rigging up your rod the same way a baseball batter takes practice swings in the on-deck circle while waiting for his turn at the plate. You'll never see a runner, baseball player or golfer take the field without warming up. Neither should you.

Do your dry casts leisurely—almost in slow motion. The more you cast, the quicker you tend to get, so think slow, right from the start of your warmups. Two other

Warm up by making some dry casts while wearing wrist weights. This builds strength and develops speed.

good warm-up exercises are trunk twisters and knee lifts. For the latter, lie on your back and punch each knee alternately to your chest and hold it there for a three-second count.

Now it's time to turn your attention to your gear. Before you tie on your terminal gear, tie on a big bank sinker and make a couple of casts to stretch out your line and get it nice and wet. Giving the line a good soaking helps get rid of memory coils and eliminates most backlash problems. When you wind the line back on the reel, check to be sure that it's at least an eighth of an inch below the flange of the spool and that the line is coming off the spool on the opposite side from where your right thumb is going to be.

Monofilament line will lose its strength quickly if left exposed to the sun too long. Check and replace line frequently, especially early in the season. Take special care to check the area where your shock leader joins the terminal tackle. That's where the most wear will occur. At the same time run an old nylon or silk stocking through your guides to check for nicks, grooves or scuffs. If it catches, replace them as soon as possible.

Cleaning and oiling your reels on a regular basis is also critical to distance casting. A good spraying with WD-40 following a tide or two of fishing will do a better job of driving out moisture and grit than a freshwater rinsing. Lubricate regularly, using a thinner oil in cold weather and a thicker one when it's hot.

And consider making or purchasing a reel cover. A good surf reel that will get you the distance you want is a major investment and it doesn't have to make many rides down the beach in the back of a 4x4 before the wear and tear starts to show. Even an old sock or a shower cap will provide some protection.

*Note: Wrist weights are used *only* to develop speed and strength during training and practice sessions for tournament competition.

5

*T*en
Tips for More Distance

I STARTED SURF FISHING AS A 12-YEAR-OLD AND I HAVEN'T looked back since, but I'm always looking for ways to learn more and improve my technique. That's probably why I got into distance casting to start with. I wondered if it would mean more fish on the beach for me, and it has. It can have the same happy benefits for you.

As we've already demonstrated in previous chapters, brute power is not part of the equation. Timing, smooth coordination of effort and use of the entire body are the major keys to success. So is the right equipment.

Some of the information in the ten tips that follow you may have read in earlier chapters, but I am repeating it here for emphasis. These suggestions are not based on tournament casting alone, but from my years of surf fishing experience as well.

------ **1** ------
THE ROD

Select a rod about 11 feet long with a fairly firm butt section and a medium-action tip. Ultra-thin-walled blanks are designed for freshwater use, but are not suited for rough and tumble surf fishing. Fiberglass remains a good choice for playing a fish, but graphite will give you better bite detection and casting distance with less effort. (See list of suppliers in an upcoming chapter).

For conventional casting, I like a reel positioned comfortably at my right-arm's length. I like a firm butt section, about six BNLG or BNHG Fuji guides, with the first gathering guide positioned at least 31 inches ahead of the reel. (In spinning make it at least 40 inches.) The first guide should be a #30 followed in order by #25, #20, #16, #12, #12, #12 ring, and a PST Fuji tip-top. Properly aligned, the guides should form a tunnel or cone (see photo). I prefer light, high-bridged guides to keep the line from slapping against the rod.

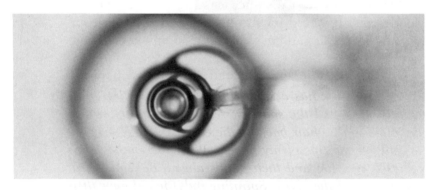

When properly aligned, guides should form a tunnel or cone that will allow the line to pass through with little resistance.

Spinning guides should be GBSVLG Fujis starting with a #40 or #50 BSHG collecting guide depending upon the size of the reel spool. The remaining guides should be Fuji GBSVLGs #30, #20, #16, #16 capped with a PLT # 16 ring Fuji tip-top.

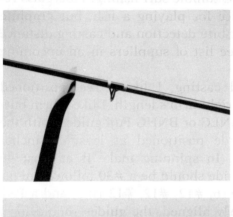

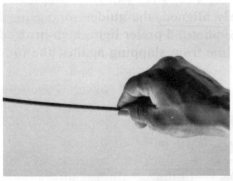

Every rod blank has a spine which will determine guide placement. I find the spine by resting the upper third of the blank on a chair back or the edge of a table and roll it between the tips of my fingers. When the blank seems to resist rotation and then jumps ahead, the spine is at the bottom of the blank. Spinning rods should have their guides mounted on the spine, while conventional casting rods work best with the guides mounted directly opposite the spine.

Whether you build your own rod or have someone else do it for you, make sure that the guides are placed on the opposite side from the spine for a conventional rod and directly on the spine for a spinning rod (almost every rod has a spine—the stiff side of the blank). This will increase the potential and release when the rod is loaded and will result in a longer cast.

------- 2 -------
THE REEL

A narrow-spooled reel will provide the greatest potential range since there is less friction as the line streams through the first guide. No anti-backlash device can replace an educated thumb on the spool's bell. When using reels with bells such as the P220 Newell, 7000 Abu or Penn 140 Squidder, train your ear as much as your thumb since a steady spin produces an even, whirring sound. Stop the spool the instant that the lure splashes down. A centrifugal brake-block or magnetically-controlled reel can help eliminate almost all manual thumbing of the spool to control backlash or overrun.

The reel should feature a tough, lightweight spool. We used to worry a lot about fracture under the pressure of memory-banked monofilament, yet this is far less a problem now than it was a decade ago. The new anodized aluminum spools and components absorb a great deal of abuse. Most mistakes now are due to "pilot error," not equipment failure.

(7 6)

-- 3 --
LINE

Monofilament line outcasts braid, for there is less friction involved in its passage through the guides. Your choice of a suitable line will be a personal matter and it is true that most of the name brands are mighty close in performance. One thing should be emphasized: always purchase a premium grade offered by a recognized firm! Never get suckered into buying "bulk" line since much of it is unstable and unreliable, often testing out heavier than the label testifies.

Fill conventional reels to within an eighth of an inch of the spool's rim—not right to the top. Leave space enough to use a thumb in feathering flow by pressure on the bell. Do not completely fill a spinning reel's spool either, for this can lead to some initial tangles.

Often, a cast is doomed before launching! It's critical to guide the line onto the spool so that it lies absolutely level. Even slight humps or bumps may slip over onto neighboring coils. This leads to the spool running at different speeds, loss of control and either disaster or shortening of the cast. Your thumb should be "educated" so that it can lay level line on your reel night or day. No secrets are involved, just a lot of practice.

The lighter the line, the longer the cast will be. Naturally, you will use a shock leader that extends back to a few turns around the reel's spool. However, some distance surfcasters tend to forget that in practical fishing one must consider the size of the species sought as well as the bottom structure to contend with. Sometimes it is necessary to sacrifice some distance in order to ensure success.

I do not usually go to ultra-light lines on Cape Cod where waters can be turbulent, bass and blues can be record sized and one must often contend with rockpiles studded with barnacles. In Cape Cod Canal, 30-pound line is a logical choice on a conventional outfit, and often you'll wish you had heavier! Twenty-pound test is about the norm in spinning. On the area's sand beaches, one can do very well with 20 or 25 on revolving spool, 12 to 15 on spinning tackle. Lighter lines guarantee longer casts, but the angler must be vigilant. Because of the line's smaller diameter, a nick can cause a breakoff and a lost fish.

---- 4 ----
LURES

We only kid ourselves when we talk about ultimate distance in the surf with anything other than aerodynamic lures. Anything that is wind-resistant will handicap the cast noticeably. The English, who often prefer to use bait instead of lures, have for that reason developed a series of torpedo-shaped sinkers with fold-out grapnel hooks and they have pioneered clever bottom rigs that keep small baits tucked in against a leader during the cast. Perhaps we go to the other extreme in our preference for artificial lures.

To achieve distance, a plug must be built to cast—or else it won't. The famous Rapala is a fish killer, but too light to achieve any distance. Lots of fine-lipped models are too wind resistant to get way out there. We need something that is admirably streamlined and properly weighted, often at the tail. This may be a popper, swimmer or other type, depending upon configuration, yet it must be designed to move through the air fluidly.

Certain metal or leadhead jigs are great in the maximum range department, but not all. You get into horizontally flattened models and they tend to plane and sail off course. Best choose the slim, compact, streamlined models: they'll shoot straight toward a far horizon. Many leadhead jigs are excellent casters and can be deadly when thrown into the edge of a boiling rip.

------------- **5** ------------
BODY MOTION

When casting, don't rely on arms and shoulders alone: use leg and hip movement to generate maximum power. Your entire body should cooperate and the movement should be well-timed and smooth. I have often likened this to the swing of a great hitter in baseball—fluid motion.

The true pendulum cast will attain greatest distance, yet it must often be varied to suit local conditions. Personally, even from an uncluttered high and dry position, I like to keep my inswing somewhat higher than most surfcasters advocate if the beach is not rubbled or if I am not working from a rockpile.

It's important to maintain balance and keep your head up. Think always of smooth, coordinated power, since the jerky, half-interrupted swing invariably produces a backlash or a short throw. Strive to be "smooth as silk." That's one of the big secrets. Get set, swing the lure behind you, feel the pendulum pull—and then come forward facing your target.

--- **6** ---
WIND

During adverse conditions against the wind, try to keep the lure trajectory low—since under those conditions a high cast will result in hampering wind resistance and a bellying of the following line. Conversely, when the wind is at your back it can be an advantage to throw high and let Mother Nature help.

-------- **7** --------
ACCURACY

Accuracy is important. At short range it becomes relatively easy to master, but at 100 yards and beyond there can be difficulty in pinpointing a target. The solution lies in constant practice: after a while the close shot becomes almost instinctive. A highly-efficient surfman is very likely to touch down in something like a ten-foot circle at 100 yards or more.

-------------------- **8** --------------------
WEATHER CONDITIONS

Wind, weather and surf conditions may help or hurt. There's no way that you'll achieve eye-popping range with a gale-force wind in your teeth, so accept that. If it seems necessary to wade, heavy surf will knock you off balance. However, under such inclement conditions, a good caster will still reach further than a neighbor who has not practiced the art. Lucky for us, many fish are apt to move closer to shore during a blow.

------------- **9** -------------
NIGHT FISHING

I see no major difference between night and day surf-casting. Techniques are precisely the same, if a bit more meticulous, after dark. The spinning outfit certainly is easiest to use at night, but anyone who has mastered the revolving spool will find that casting becomes almost instinctive. The line is laid properly by that educated thumb and the whole operation becomes more feel than vision. On the darkest of nights you can hedge your bets by wearing a small penlight on a cord around your neck to illuminate the reel while retrieving.

------- **10** -------
PRACTICE

Practice! Maybe this sounds obvious, yet it is one of the keys to success. Visit the fishing grounds whenever you can, but practice in all seasons. There are folks who make snide remarks when they see casters throwing unarmed weights on football fields or deserted beaches during the chill winter months, conveniently forgetting that these enthusiasts are honing their own skills.

There is no quick and easy road to success: indeed it is hard work. It took me ten years before I thought I was ready for tournament competition, yet it surely paid off. Now I can throw pretty well and have won four Stren National Longcasting Championships.

But more important than that, I'm a better fisherman through an appreciation of tackle and a better understanding of techniques. You can be too.

6

Rigging
for that
Faraway Fish

AS WE POINTED OUT IN THE INTRODUCTION, THIS BOOK is about long-distance fishing, not long-distance casting. The modified pendulum cast wasn't developed to win Distance Casting titles; it was developed because striped bass were feeding in the middle of the Cape Cod Canal and outside the Sandwich bar and there was no other way to reach them.

Obviously you're not going to be able to throw a gob of clams with a heavy pyramid sinker on a fishfinder rig four or five hundred feet and have it arrive in one piece. But there are some bait rigs that work better than others, two of which are illustrated here.

Most of the long-distance fishing done in the United States is done with jigs or lures, the more aerodynamic in design the better. I like to tie them right to the shock leader with a palomar knot or use a snap without a swivel. I find that this gives the lure a better action. When I'm jigging bucktails for striped bass in the Cape Cod Canal, which has some vicious currents that can tangle lines, I'll tie in a barrel swivel about two feet ahead of the jig. If you do this, make sure to use a

On the pages that follow is a gallery of my favorite surf-casting lures, both for their "castability" and their effectiveness in catching fish.

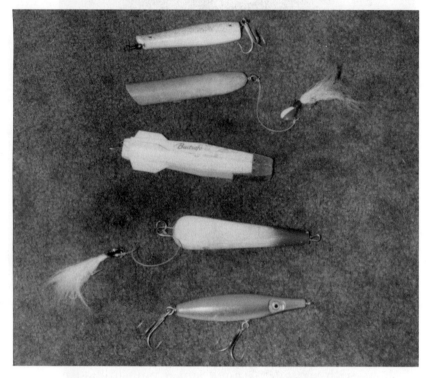

Top to bottom: A Gag's Grabber "Bluefish Bomb," 1.7 oz. Good for surface-feeding fish, this can be retrieved slow or fast. Casts very well for a light-weight surface lure.

A 2 oz. Atom Popper with a ³/₈ oz. bucktail jig. A light lure good for rough water, this should be retrieved slowly.

English-style "Baitsafe" lure, 4 oz. Use this as a bottom rig, with sea worms. This lure hits the water and opens up to let bait fall out.

Three-ounce Atom Ketch n' Fetch with a ³/₈ oz. bucktail lead-head jig.

Super Strike Bullet, 1-⁵/₈ oz. Good for reaching beyond the sandbars at daylight for feeding fish.

Top to bottom: Stan Gibbs 3-1/4 oz. Polaris Popper, excellent for feeding bass at daybreak. Casts like a rocket.

Roberts lure, 4 oz. One of my favorite bluefish lures.

Atom Popper, "Swingin' Swiper," 2 oz. Great for stripers and bluefish. Single hook aids in catch-and-release.

Stan Gibbs Pencil Popper, 3 oz. Good, all-around surface lure that does well in fast-moving water. Best used at daybreak and just before dark.

Creek Chub Popper, 2-1/8 oz. Another good all-around surface lure, this one makes noisy "pops" to attract feeding fish.

(8 7)

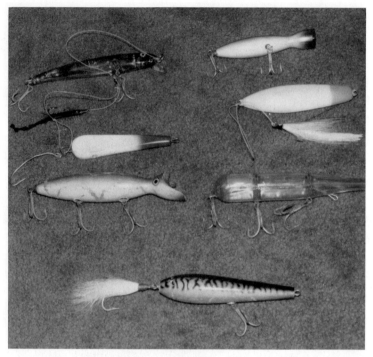

Clockwise from upper left: Bomber Lure swimmer, 7" and 1-1/2 oz., with an Eddystone eel dropper. I've caught hundreds of striped bass with this lure, most at night. It casts very well for a light swimming lure.

Super-Strike Little Neck Popper. Best at early-morning tides and before dark, this casts well with little effort.

4-oz. Roberts lure with bucktail streamer. Great for casting into the wind.

3-1/2 oz. Reverse Atom Lure. Great when fish are feeding on squid, this can be used night or day.

Stan Gibbs skipper lure, 2-3/4 oz. Aerodynamically shaped for excellent casting. Works well in fast-moving water.

Stan Gibbs swimmer lure, 3 oz. Very good for large fish or when fish are feeding on large baitfish like menhaden or porgies.

Atom Ketch –n' Fetch, 3 oz.

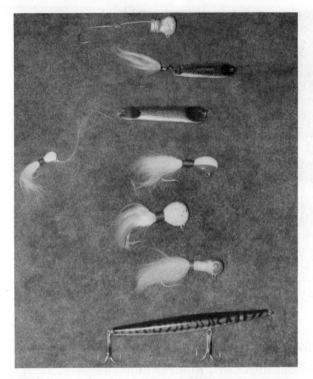

Top to bottom: Single-hook eelskin rig, 3-$\frac{1}{2}$ oz. Best cast against the current and bounced along the bottom. Pork rind can be added to the hook.

"Shorty" Hopkins Lure, 2-$\frac{1}{4}$ oz. Can be used any time of day, though I usually use this when the weather is rough.

4-$\frac{1}{2}$ oz. Hopkins with $\frac{3}{8}$ bucktail jig.

Bill Upperman jig, 2 oz., does well when used with pork rind on hook. This bucktail will catch any species of fish. The US Navy even includes it in its survival kits!

Lead-head bucktail, 5 oz. A great casting lure, this can be used with pork rind on the hook. Good for fast-moving currents.

Lead-head bucktail, 3 oz.

Super Strike "Needle Fish," 1-$\frac{3}{4}$ oz. Good at night and in swift-moving water. Should be retrieved very slowly.

(8 9)

Clockwise from upper left: Eelskin rig, double-tandem hook, 4 oz. Good for fast currents.

Official "Aquazoom" tournament distance-casting sinker, 5-1/4 oz.

Cape Hatteras Hurricane sinker, 8 oz. Used in bottom fishing when fast currents and strong tides are present.

English-style sinker, 6 oz., with swivelling grip wires. This is used for bottom fishing on sand and gravel bottoms in fast currents.

Bank sinker, 4-1/2 oz. Used in rocks or reefs.

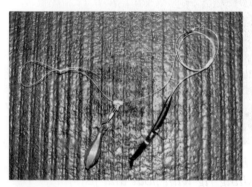

Fishfinder rig with bank sinker and eddystone eel. This rig can be cast over 400 feet and works well in fast currents.

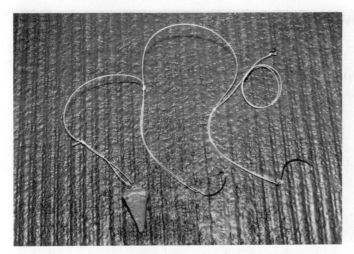

*High-low rig with 6-oz. pyramid sinker with wide-gap
4/0 hooks. I often use this rig with fresh sand eels, fishing
on a sandy bottom.*

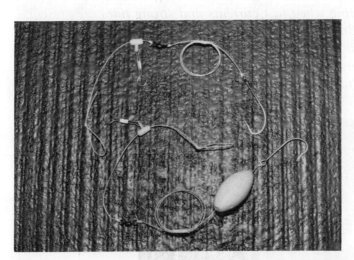

*Top: Standard cut-bait bottom rig, without float.
Bottom: Bottom-fishing rig with float and fish-finder rig.
The float keeps bait off the bottom where skate and other
bottom-feeding fish can steal bait away from game fish.*

swivel that will stand up to the kinetic energy produced by the pendulum cast.

I normally use 15 to 17-pound test running line behind my 50-pound shock leader. The best way to connect the two is to tie a half hitch in the shock leader, run the lighter line through and tighten snugly, tie a Uni-knot with the lighter line around the shock leader, wet both lines and pull the knots until they tighten and butt up against one another. This makes a nice, compact connection that slides through the guides easily.

Once you've gotten the lure where you want it, long distance casting gives way to long distance fishing. Remember that you've got 300 or 400 feet of stretchy monofilament between you and your lure or bait. It's important to keep a tight line in order to be able to feel a strike.

And when you do feel that hit, don't try to set the hook. Even with a tight line there will be too much stretch to do that effectively. Wait until the fish has hooked itself and started to take line. And it goes without saying that your hooks should be sharp enough to catch on your thumbnail.

FILLING A REVOLVING-SPOOL REEL

Insert a pencil into the supply spool to allow the fishing line to feed smoothly off the spool. Have someone hold each end of the pencil while you turn the reel handle. Keep proper tension on the line by having the person holding the pencil exert a slight inward pressure on the supply spool. *Courtesy DuPont Stren*

NOTE: keep line level when retrieving line.

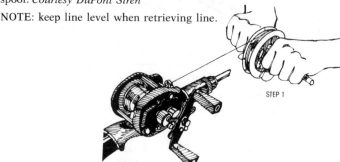

STEP 1

FILLING A SPINNING REEL

You fill a spinning/open-face reel differently than a bait-casting reel because you must allow for the rotation of the pick-up bail which may cause the line to twist.

Follow these steps:

1. Have someone hold the supply spool or place it on the floor or ground.

2. Pull the line so that it spirals (balloons) off the end of the spool.

3. Thread the line through the rod guides and tie the line to the reel with the bail in the open position. Hold the rod tip three to four feet away from the supply spool. Make fifteen to twenty turns on the reel handle, then stop.

4. Check for line twist by moving the rod tip to about one foot from the supply spool. If the slack line twists, turn the supply spool completely around. This will eliminate most of the twist as you wind the rest of the line onto the reel.

5. Always keep a light tension on fishing line when spooling any reel. Do this by holding the line between the thumb and forefinger of your free hand.

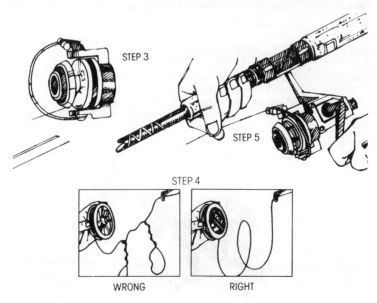

PALOMAR KNOT

This is my favorite knot for large hook eyes, sinker eyes, and tournament sinker connections. *Courtesy DuPont Stren.*

1. Double about 4 inches of line and pass loop through eye.

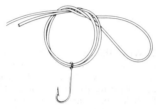

2. Let hook hang loose and tie overhand knot in doubled line. Avoid twisting the lines and don't tighten.

3. Pull loop of line far enough to pass it over hook, swivel or lure. Make sure loop passes completely over this attachment.

4. Pull both tag end and standing line to tighten. Clip tag end.

This knot is equally as good as the Improved Clinch for terminal tackle connections and is easier to tie, except when using large plugs. It, too, is used by most of the pros.

IMPROVED CLINCH KNOT

I use this knot for small hook eyes, lure eyes, and swivels. It's quick and simple to tie. *Courtesy DuPont Stren.*

This is a good knot for making terminal-tackle connections and is best used for lines up to 20-pound test. It is a preferred knot by professional fishermen and angling authorities.

1. Pass line through eye of hook, swivel, or lure. Double back and make five turns around the standing line. Hold coils in place; thread end of line around first loop above the eye, then through big loop as shown.

2. Hold tag end and standing line while coils are pulled up. Take care that coils are in spiral, not lapping over each other. Slide tight against eye. Clip tag end.

(9 4)

ALBRIGHT SPECIAL

I use the Albright for tying a leader to a lighter main line and for tying mono to wire. When you need a strong knot, this is the best. *Courtesy DuPont Stren.*

1. Double back a couple inches of the heavy line and insert about 10 inches of the light line through the loop in the heavy line.

2. Wrap the light line back over itself and over both strands of the heavy line. While doing this you are gripping the light line and both leader strands with the thumb and finger of your left hand, and winding with your right.

3. Make ten turns, then insert the end of the line back through the loop once more at the point of original entry.

4. Pull gently on both ends of heavy line sliding knot toward loop. Remove slack by pulling on standing and tag ends of light line. Pull both standing lines as tight as possible and clip off excess from both tag ends.

JOINING LINES

This is a variation on the Uni Knot and an excellent small-diameter knot for attaching the shock leader to the main line.

STEP 1
OVERHAND KNOT

STEP 2
UNI-KNOT LOOP
SHOCK LEADER
MAIN LINE

1. Overlap ends of two lines of about the same diameter for about 6 inches. With one end, form Uni-Knot circle, crossing the two lines about midway of overlapped distance.

STEP 3
PULL OVERHAND KNOT TIGHT
PULL UNI-KNOT TIGHT AND SLIDE
AGAINST OVERHAND KNOT
WET THE LINE WITH SPIT SO KNOT
SLIDES BETTER

2. Tie basic Uni-Knot, making six turns around the two lines.

(9 5)

TOURNAMENT CASTING KNOT

Another variation on the Uni-knot, this one employs a burr melted onto the tip of the shock leader to prevent the smaller-diameter main line from slipping. Keep this burr as small as possible to minimize the friction as it moves through the guides.

If you are connecting very light monofilament to a heavy leader, use a match or cigarette lighter to create a burr on the tag end of the heavy leader. Keep the burr small, but bulky enough to prevent the light line from slipping over it.

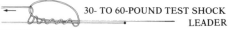

1. Overlap ends of two lines of about the same diameter for about 6 inches. With one end, form Uni-Knot circle, crossing the two lines about midway of overlapped distance.

30- TO 60-POUND TEST SHOCK
LEADER

12- TO 17-POUND TEST MAIN LINE

2. Tie basic Uni-Knot, making six turns around the two lines.

PULL AND SLIDE TO BUMP AGAINST BURR

SNIP TO 1/32"

7

*T*he
Tournament
Trail

S OONER OR LATER, IN ANY SPORT, THE SPECTER OF competition raises its shaggy head. Nobody with any kind of athletic background (and yes, fishermen *are* athletes) can resist the temptation to find out just how good he or she really is. Distance Casting tournaments are the place to find out.

In the United States most tournaments allow each caster six attempts and count the longest of the six that lands in-bounds. All competitors are required to use a 50-pound shock leader. Standard sinker weight in the United States is 5¼ ounces.

Sportcast USA sponsors a series of tournaments in spring and early summer up and down the Atlantic seaboard which is climaxed with the National Championships, generally at Lewes, Delaware, every October. There are many local competitions as well. It's a good idea to take in a couple of events as a spectator before you decide to make the investment in equipment and practice time that it takes to become a serious tournament caster.

And we're talking a serious investment. Tournament

rod blanks start at around $300 and go upwards from there. You'll need two or three modified reels, which we'll discuss in depth later, and there are hidden costs such as the cost of replacing line. Consider that every

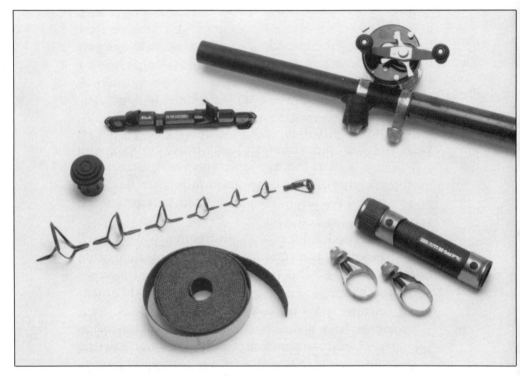

Some of the components of a tournament casting rod (clockwise from upper left hand corner): FS-7SB Fuji reel seat, Abu 6000C mounted on rod butt with English reel clamps (note the reducer fitted into the end of the rod butt behind the reel), FPSD Fuji reel seat, English reel clamps, ¹/₃₂-inch cork tape, Fuji BNLG guides for conventional rods, rubber butt cap.

time you backlash (and even the best of us do that a
lot) 300 yards of new line generally has to go back on
the reel. You'll go through a 1000-yard spool of line in
a hurry if you put in as much practice time as you
should.

As we've already mentioned in the introduction,
tournament Distance Casting equipment is designed
specifically for competition. Most serious tournament
casters use competition blanks made in England by
Zziplex. They range from 13½ to 14 feet in length with
a very limber tip and an extremely stiff butt section.
You can order them ready-made, but most casters prefer to attach their own guides and rod clamp, spacing
them to suit their particular style. Casters with small
hands will need a reducer, a 12-inch length of smaller-
diameter fiberglass that fits onto the rod butt and holds
the reel while allowing the caster to get a firm grip and
apply pressure on the reel spool with the left hand and
thumb.

You won't find very many larger diameter, revolving
spool salt water reels on a tournament casting field.
Most serious competitors start with smaller bait casting reels equipped with some sort of magnetic anti-
backlash device and then make some simple standard
modifications. My tournament reels are 6000C centrifugal brakeblock Garcia, Ultra-Mag XL3s which have had
the level-wind mechanism replaced with a solid cross-
bar, and the top bar removed for better thumb grip,
and with four of the eight magnets in the anti-backlash
mechanism removed. I make adjustment (more on that
later) easier by gluing a small cork to the backlash control button on the left side of the reel. Other tournament casters use caps from toothpaste tubes which
work just as efficiently.

The reel is also positioned differently on a tournament rod. Instead of being in the normal position halfway along the grip, it is clamped in place six inches

The Abu Garcia Ultra Mag III and 6000C reels are favored by most tournament distance casters. The Ultra Mag III spool and side plate are at left. Note the cork glued to the side plate to adjust the magnets while the sinker is in flight. The 6000C at right utilizes centrifugal brake blocks to prevent overruns. Both reels have been modified by having their level-wind mechanisms removed.

from the end of the reducer with English-style screw clamps and the reel is released with the left thumb rather than the right. There should be just enough room below the reel for the left hand to grip the reducer.

Before we get into the cast itself, let's talk about safety for a minute. On a 700-foot cast the sinker is leaving my rod tip at speeds of close to 200 miles an hour. It's going faster than that on a break-off which means that for all intents and purposes, it's a 5¼-ounce bullet. Keep that in mind when you pick a place to practice.

SETTING UP—Before I start to the cast I make it a point to double check my reel set-up. My left thumb is covered (up to the tip) by a neoprene rubber thumb guard (I cut it from an old Arctic glove) that has ridges so that the reel will not slip under the tremendous amount of pressure I'm creating during the cast until I'm ready to release the line. The line should leave from the right side of the reel, opposite from where my thumb will rest, with three turns of the shock leader around the arbor of the reel and the shocker knot (connecting the shock leader and running line) tucked in at the right side of the spool. The reel should be filled to within 1/16th of an inch of the top, on a tournament reel.

A thumb guard is essential to keep the spool from slipping prior to release of the tournament pendulum cast. Mine is made from a finger cut from an old Arctic glove.

(103)

THE TOURNAMENT CAST

The starting position. My left hand is wrapped around the reducer with my thumb on the reel spool and my index finger around the reel clamp. The rod butt is tucked under my right armpit and my right hand is extended up the rod as far as possible, holding the rod at a 45-degree angle.

The start of the outswing. I'm holding the rod almost vertically and tipping it out slightly with my right hand to start the sinker in motion. Note that the outswing is more exaggerated here than in the other casts we've described, but it still goes no higher than the tip of the rod. This is possible because of better traction which I enhance even further by wearing athletic shoes with ¼-inch rubber cleats.

Now I've started the inswing by pulling up gently with my right hand and pushing down with my left to bring the sinker behind me.

The sinker is at the apex of the inswing, high above and at right angles to the rod tip and I'm feeling that little tug that signals that it is starting to load the rod. Most of my weight is still on my right foot.

Starting the cast. I'm using my body and turning my shoulders to start pulling the rod toward the target and in the opposite direction of the sinker. My left leg moves more to the left and my weight is beginning to transfer. Notice that my head is leading my body into the cast. At this point I'm telling myself: "Don't hurry. Take it real slow."

The rod is approaching full lock and building up speed. I'm using my hips and body to bring the rod around and up into the lever position, punching up with my right hand and pulling down with my left.

The point of release. The rod comes over the top at a 45 degree angle to create a javelin effect enhanced by the punch up-pull down lever action of my hands. The key at this point is to keep the rod tip pointed at the sinker so that the line flows smoothly through the guides. Even the slightest bit of friction here will reduce distance dramatically.

FEATHERING THE CAST—If there's one thing that you never do under any circumstances in a tournament cast it's to thumb the reel once the sinker is on its way. That's a quick ticket to the biggest backlash you'll ever see and a certain break-off.

I start turning the cork attached to the Ultra Mag XL3 backlash control button clockwise when the sinker has been on its way for two seconds to keep the reel from over-running as the sinker starts to slow down. This is an art that takes a lot of practice and you'll get your share of backlashes, but keep at it until it's second nature. Sometimes it's that little bit of reel-turning that will translate into those two or three extra inches that will win a tournament.

Appendix

SOURCES FOR EQUIPMENT

Rods for Distance Casting Tournaments

Carroll Laminates, Unit 2, Mountfield Road, Industrial Estate, New Romney Kent, TN28 8LY, ENGLAND

Sinkers Designed for Distance

D.C.A. Moulds, SA4 The Maltings, East Tyndall Street, Cardiff, CF1 5EA, ENGLAND

Distance Rods for Fishing

Abu Garcia, Inc., 21 Law Drive, Fairfield, NJ 07004 (201) 227-7666
Daiwa Corp., 7421 Chapman Avenue, Garden Grove, CA 92641 (714) 895-6645
Fenwick, 5242 Argosy Drive, Huntington Beach, CA 92649 (714) 897-1066

Lamiglas, P.O. Box U, Woodland, WA 98674 (206) 225-9436

Penn Fishing Tackle Manufacturing Company, 3028 West Hunting Park Avenue, Philadelphia, PA 19132 (215) 229-9415

St. Croix Rods, P.O. Box 279, Park Falls, WI 54552 (715) 762-3236

Reels for Distance Casting

Abu Garcia, Inc., 21 Law Drive, Fairfield, NJ 07004 (201) 227-7666

Daiwa Corp., 7421 Chapman Avenue, Garden Grove, CA 92641 (714) 895-6645

Carl W. Newell Mfg., 940 Allen Avenue, Glendale, CA 91201 (213) 245-9641

Penn Fishing Tackle Manufacturing Company, 3028 West Hunting Park Avenue, Philadelphia, PA 19132 (215) 229-9415

Shimano American Corporation, One Shimano Drive, Irvine, CA 92718 (714) 951-5003

Zebco, P.O. Box 270, Tulsa, OK 74101 (918) 836-5581

TOURNAMENT RULES

Distance-casting tournaments in the United States are sanctioned by Sportcast USA and we reprint some of its rules for casting competition below. Other rules cover formation of clubs, judging, awards, and more. For full information contact Sportcast USA, 148 S. DuPont Parkway, New Castle, DE 19720.

Rules reprinted courtesy Sportcast USA.

Outfit

A. CONVENTIONAL TACKLE:
   1. Rod: There shall be no restriction upon length or on the material used in its construction.
   2. Reel: To contain a revolving spool and be of standard manufacture, commonly available to the general public.
      a. No alterations or machining to deviate from the original design and manufacture of the spool.
      b. Bearings may be replaced only with equal quality and size as the original.

B. SPINNING TACKLE:
   1. Rod: Same as for conventional tackle.
   2. Reel: To contain a spool that is fixed during the cast. It must be of standard manufacture and commonly available to the general public. Modifications are allowed except for the following:
      a. Spools may not be altered in any way from original design and manufacture.

C. LINE:
   1. Running Line: All casters shall use line of no less that .35 mm test in all events. The line shall be of the same diameter and parallel throughout the entire length.
   2. Shock Line: To be no less than .75 mm test in all events, for all casters. At least five (5) turns of shock leader must be around the spool of any reel before any cast shall be attempted. Shock leaders shall be parallel throughout their entire length.

D. CASTING WEIGHTS:
1. Men shall cast a 5-¼ oz. weight, of a design approved by SPORTCAST USA, in all team events.
2. Women shall cast a 4-½ oz. weight, of a design approved by SPORTCAST USA in all team events.
3. Men shall cast a 5-¼ oz. weight in an individual long cast event.
4. Women shall cast a 4-½ oz. weight in a individual long cast event.
5. All weights shall have the size clearly marked and may not be altered by cutting, shaving, filing, or excessive polishing.

Events

A. TEAM:
1. A team shall consist of no more than (5) casters.
2. Each caster shall make five casts for the team.
3. The team that totals the greatest combined distance shall be declared the winner of this event.
4. In the event of a tie between teams, each member of each team shall make one cast; the team whose five casts total the greatest distance shall be declared the winner.

B. INDIVIDUAL: LONG CAST
1. Each man shall make six (6) casts with a 5-¼ oz. casting weight. Each woman shall make six (6) casts with a 4-½ oz. casting weight. Only the longest cast of the six (6) will be considered for awards.
2. Junior casters, 12 to 18 years of age, shall make six (6) casts with a 4-½ oz. casting weight. Sub-Junior caster, under the age of 12, shall make

(1 1 8)

six (6) casts with a 2 oz. casting weight. Only the longest cast of the six (6) will be considered for awards.

3. In the event of a tie, each caster in the tie shall make one (1) cast with the longest declared the winner.

C. ALL EVENTS:
1. A caster in any event may cast with the outfit of his/her choice; spinning or conventional tackle.
2. Each caster shall choose the desired tackle when registering for an event and may not change for the duration of that event.
3. No re-entries are permitted in any event.

Field

A. GRADE: The grade of the casting field shall not exceed eight (8) feet in eight hundred (800) feet.
B. CASTING COURT: A thirty (30) degree casting court will be used at all tournaments. The casting court shall be laid out in the following manner: A base line pin shall be driven in the ground and a center line extended as necessary. From this pin, side lines shall be extended out at a fifteen (15) degree angle from the center line to the same length as the center line. At 100 meters (328 feet 10 inches) the field will be 51.76 meters (169 feet 9.75 inches) wide. We will use a casting mat 8 feet 2.5 inches by 8 feet 2.5 inches square, with an 8 feet 2.5 inches by ¾ inch by 4 inch boardset at cast line.
C. CASTING ZONE: There shall be a safety zone established in back of the base line. This zone shall be fifty (50) feet deep for a distance of at least one hundred and fifty (150) feet on each side of the center

line and be clearly marked. No person shall be allowed inside this safety zone except the one that is about to cast.

Measurement of Casts

A. All casts will be measured by the radial method directly from the center of the base line. If a full length tape is not available, measurements may be made from cross lines set at 100 feet intervals. These lines shall be set in an arc form one side line to the other. The measuring tape shall be set at a 90 degree angle to the arc of the cross line. An electronic measuring device may also be used (E.M.D.).

B. All casts shall be measured to the farthest extremity of the lead weight. All casts shall be measured as they are found.

C. A steel or fiberglass tape shall be used to measure all casts of an E.M.D.

D. PENALTIES:

   1. Break-off will be scored as "zero." A break-off occurs when any line breaks after the power phase of a cast has begun until the casting weight has come to rest on the ground.

   2. A base line foul shall result in a fifty (50) feet deduction from the measured length of the cast. A caster has fouled when any portion of his/her body touches the ground ahead of the base line.

   3. A casting weight landing outside the side lines shall be considered as out of bounds. All casts determined to be out of bounds will be scored a "zero."

Methods of Casting

A. All casters shall cast forward from behind the base

line in a designated area. No caster shall pass this base line while in the act of casting and until the casting weight has landed.

B. It shall not be permitted to make any cast with a power stroke of more than 360 degrees or any cast that is determined by the tournament officials to be dangerous.

C. Each caster will be given a number for each event. A caster will be called to cast in numerical order and must do so unless excused by a tournament official.

D. After a cast is completed, a caster must place his/her rod on the ground ahead of the base line or in a designated area set aside by tournament officials.

E. No person, except an official, may precede the casters as they follow their lines to reach their casting weights.

Index

Note: page numbers in italics refer to illustrations